Isa the Truck Named Isadore

Isa the Truck
Named Isadore

POEMS

Amanda Nadelberg

Winner of the 2005
Slope Editions Book Prize

SLOPE EDITIONS

New Hampshire • New York • Massachusetts

COPYRIGHT © 2006 Amanda Nadelberg
COVER & BOOK DESIGN Linda S. Koutsky
COVER PHOTOGRAPH © Amanda Nadelberg
AUTHOR PHOTOGRAPH © Hannah E. Kaplan

LIBRARY OF CONGRESS
CATALOGING-IN-PUBLICATION DATA

Nadelberg, Amanda.
Isa the truck named Isadore : poems / Amanda Nadelberg.—1st ed.
p. cm.
"Winner of the 2005 Slope Editions Book Prize."
ISBN 0-9777698-0-1 (alk. paper)
I. Title.

PS3614.A28173 2006
811'.6—DC22

2006002606

FIRST EDITION | FIRST PRINTING
1 3 5 7 9 8 6 4 2

Printed in the United States

In "Karp," the phrase "She was truly a lovely ripe peach,
nectarine, whatever" is borrowed and slightly altered
from *Hotel Lambosa,* by Kenneth Koch.

ACKNOWLEDGMENTS

Some of these poems appeared in *The Canary, Conduit, jubilat, Konundrum Engine Literary Review, No: a journal of the arts, Octopus, Pindeldyboz, Slope, Spout, Tarpaulin Sky,* and *Typo*. Thank you to the editors of those journals.

I am so glad for *A Dictionary of First Names* (courtesy of Oxford University Press), my steady reading companion for seven months.

Thank you, Chris Fischbach, thank you. Thank you Adam Clay, Sarah Fox and Dobby Gibson, for helping. Thank you Greg Hewett. Thanks, too, to Cris Mattison. Thanks to the kind folks of Slope Editions. Thank you Linda Koutsky. And thank you Lisa Jarnot.

And this is where I get to thank my family, and my friends, my best friends. This is where I get to say how nice they all are. They are all so nice and they are lots of ages. Like how Ollie is eighty-five. Tara is twenty-four, while Kyra is only twenty-three. Oshi and Brianna fall somewhere in between. And Alexander, Alexander is two.

For Nay and Mike
and Daniel and Sara

Contents

Isa the Truck Named Isadore

G REAT TALENT gravitates to and from the center of Minnesota; it's true. Think of Bob Dylan or James Wright or Jack Spicer. And these great minds think alike, plotting out a graph of the absurdity of the human condition—the things that make human beings special—our frailties and foibles and our constant efforts to make sense of the materials of the world as they shoot past us on highways and streets and through our own living rooms. This is what I think of when I read Amanda Nadelberg's poems—that she is a writer who pulls these moments of American chaos from the air to neatly precisely joyously record them. She does it lovingly, with wit, and best of all with an incredible attention to the subtle twists that language takes around us. This is where it all begins: "Adelaide / was walking on / her own street when / a bird flew in / to her forehead / like to Fabio / on that roller coaster." I think that this is the stuff that life is made of. I'm sad for Adelaide and for Fabio, but they will survive (as much as any of us will), and could it also be delightful that life is filled with this quality of surprise? To quote Robert Creeley quoting a greeting card he once received "Expect the unexpected / And have a happy day."

It seems likely, reader, that you will have a happy day reading this book. Perhaps you can take to heart the fact that this excellent young poet from Boston (who currently works in an organic ice cream store in Minnesota and who has the gift of first-rate word-smithing) has come to entertain you in this special way. Perhaps too her work will bring to mind the catalogue-frenzied travels of Christopher Smart in his epic *Jubilate Agno*. Think of the names of all of the people you've ever known, called up in a great alphabetical roll call outside the pearly gates or at a rest stop in Ohio waiting to meet Miss America. Think of the human ability to express tender love and tender uncertainty and tender bewilderment and think of Wallace Stevens and how

i

he must have felt about the cat in the grass in "A Rabbit as King of the Ghosts." Maybe you will never know exactly what he meant, but it felt good to read it, and you were ultimately satisfied, like Wallace Stevens' cat was ultimately satisfied: "Fat cat, red tongue, green mind, white milk." Think too of Gertrude Stein's grammatical constructions—turns of phrase that may remind you that there is a language that is native to you and it is kind of weird. Amanda Nadelberg writes: "Love the white things the / paper towels the milk the / sky sometimes." Someone is speaking to you. All those people who you ride with on the subway, who you stand in line with at the supermarket in the afternoon. Maybe they have names like this. Maybe you will find yourself here, or your neighbors, or the people who you love. Maybe Amanda Nadelberg has captured some satisfying "truth" about our lives as people, as twenty-first century Americans, as the children that we are, with our talk shows and our presidents and the Red Sox.

There are sixty-three stories in this book of poetry: stories of the naming of peoples in the traditions of the Teutons and the Greeks and the Jews. Imagine all of this information presented to you with a carefulness of what we poets refer to as our prosody: hot prosody, singing sounds, graceful leaps of the lines, well shaped couplets, conversational dexterity—almost eerie in its Rimbaudian perfection. It's delightful—this poet is the antenna of the race. Tune in here.

—Lisa Jarnot, June 2005

Isa the Truck Named Isadore

Adelaide

Was walking on
her own street when
a bird flew in
to her forehead
like to Fabio
on that roller coaster
when he came out
all bloody—for Fabio
it had been for
promotional purposes
except the blood and
the bird—a mistake—
he was mad—
for Adelaide it
was sad her mother
worked outside the
home her mother
was a person in
an office and not
home to clean up
Adelaide's head
which was red from
all the blood from
all of the bird.

This is why I love you.
This and this and this.

Albert

Two whole light bulbs are too much
for one room on certain occasions that
are to occur biweekly. Here is where
you cough and I say god bless
you lovely. Four and four and
four is twelve napkins. Follow
me through lunchtime in the
city I will walk you from the
bus stop to the bus stop there is
a chair on the corner if you
want some resting. I look cool because
this here is a white turtleneck and
I learned how to mow the lawn with
this bicycle. I'll leave a crack
in the ceiling for you darling.

Anona

All the wrong ways
of bringing a bag
lunch make this
something that we need
to end something
that is green and
white together in
a coat closet in
some piece of
New Jersey.
Shhh. The
hangers are sleeping.

Audrey

The trees are growing faster these days
because the wind and the trees are in
cahoots. The blue shirt looks much
nicer with those shoes. You have seen
Niagara Falls when it was almost
empty of those people in love. I would
like to see it like that. The
trees at first didn't believe the
sun when she said the winds were
dealing. But soon they saw what it had
done for the grass and the moon and
in May they sat down together. It was
something about dinnertime and speed
and song. The ratio is almost perfect
and one day it will be even better.

Bean

Inside this small
place I can
love you. Let me
wash your hair in
the bathroom sink and
make you a glass
of water with many
cubes I promise they
will fit. Even though my
new ice trays are being
difficult I wouldn't
mind making more
for you Beanie.

Blodwen

Green and purple and blue she
said would be the colors of
the party. And the cat said
green and purple and blue. The
town decided that stop signs
were going unnoticed so they began a
campaign—painting them otherwise—
some yellow some orange some pink.
People started paying notice and
every day became an ice cream day.

The following is the benediction.

If you come to a place
in the road where there is
not one but you gather there
might have been, then be a dear
and pretend there is—any color you like.

Cadogan

How comforting to find yourself
viewing a tele program that you
have witnessed before. And
you Cadogan what are
you doing over there
with the shovel and
the chair? Do you like
the chair? Do you like
to sit on the shovel?
Does the chair like the
shovel? If you break this
car you'll have to go
home on the paddy wagon
shameful with the shovel or the
chair not the two. You will
need one hand to keep
in your pocket. There you'll find
comfort in warmth and quiet.
There is no tele on the paddy wagon.
You may find the quiet to
be nice. Otherwise unpleasant. Here
is to a long line of your descendents
may they all be quiet and
warm with hands full of pockets.

Carwyn

Love the white things the
paper towels the milk the
sky sometimes. Take water
and sand separately into your
mouth. Read them more
times than you really wish to.
Go to a small box and speak
to the religious attendant of
your choice. A broom will
do wonders. Pick me up
when I ring. Carry these
phone books upstairs your
mother doesn't need to. Feel
this—do you—the vibrations in
my knees. Build two kitchens there
will be less mess than if there is
only one. One downstairs
one up. Tell me what
you're thinking. Please do.

Cecil

Cecil an old man responsible
for functions and fundraisers. He wore
handkerchiefs in his coat pockets. Cecil
curated an excellent library along
with a garden. People should not
keep trying to grow grass under pines
he said. He said there are plenty
of flowers that would do quite
well under pine trees. People are
too partial to grass Cecil would say.

Ceridwen

Read "Carwyn"
again but with feeling.

Cheslav

The only place my mom
takes me is the dentist.

Clelia

My wedding was in the
bay. My parents hired the
National Bench Association to
make enough floatable benches
for our one hundred and six friends.
That is twenty-six benches. It was
nice how we were all together
but not on top of one another or
in control of the benches. They
were plain pine benches. No one
wore shoes. Well they wore them
to get to the bay but then
they left them on the dock like
a coat check I guess. Like that
episode where Carrie loses her
400-dollar Manolo Blahniks. I like
the coat check at the Museum of
Fine Arts in Boston. So
we were exchanging the niceties we
had written for the ceremony and one
of our friends, Marilyn, fell in. She
was sharing a bench with our friends
with larger asses. Marilyn is tiny she
was barely holding on. Marilyn's
husband couldn't swim so he didn't
go in after her but the Rabbi did—he was
an excellent swimmer and a good Rabbi.
A slight delay in the service but

we were all just so happy
that Mar was okay. Her
husband was especially happy he
told the Rabbi if he ever needed
life insurance he should
call right up—he sold it and
could get him a good price.

Cuthbert

Today is so sad today. The
man at the post office asked me
for small bills I had none he
asked if I could put the five
dollars on a credit card and I
refused. It's not like he
offered to pay the bill. My
parents are gone and I am
glad about it. I spend so much
of myself reading lips and
I have difficulty with reading
comprehension. My table consists
of flowers I'm trying to kill
and small pencils. I don't know
where the supermarkets are and I
need to make dinner for you and
for me mostly. I am concerned
for the election and for walking too
loudly. And fitting both legs into
one pant. That could make
things better.

Daisy

I have brown hair and when I was
little I swam a whole lot on a team and
all the chlorine would make my hair so
light in the summer people called it
dirty blonde and I was. For years I've been
keeping a tally of my showers. Many showers
for many years. People may think it's
strange but some people think about
their mothers while they're plowing
some lady and that's worse. Don't
you think all of us keep tally
of something? Light bulbs, sexes,
ice creams, episodes, houses, stars.
Let Daisy be in her little white dress on
a big blue lawn it doesn't really
matter what she's doing.

Deforest

Pennsylvania is sort of big compared to a child but
that is not really the point here. The point is that
the president, in my dream, was making a lewd
gesture, pointing towards my body and I thought,
we've got him. He's totally cooked. Someone write
the book about how he is so over—we are all over it.
This new expression, I guess it means "I have stopped
loving you" because people on TV are using it and
the woman in the store today, she used it too. We are
all over it, we say collectively, we.
One day it was something that no one
said and the next it's on the television and
there is nothing, not one thing wrong with learning
from the fine people on television. They
obviously did something great to get there, so
if you try harder you will be over it too.

Dottie

Like those people who
wash their hands
too much God
may need to come
down for blackberries
every now and again.

Dymphna

The glove salesman is coming the
glove salesman is coming to sell
us gloves because it is time
for gloves soon. He has
purple hands and little teeth
and he wants to meet you. He
says you are just going to love
the new collection. Red ones and
green ones and gray ones and
black ones and he's really a
lovely person the way he brings
everything in such small packages.
I think I'm going to write his
employer a note to say what a
lovely glove salesman he is how
he always likes my cookies and
thinks to pat the dog. He just
makes you feel like
and like everything's beautiful.

Ebba

Tell her I want to apologize
like the talk show with the
four ladies said. I learned
from the four ladies that nothing
is worth fighting about. I can
forgive her now for putting golf
balls in my shower and peacocks
in the oven. The peacocks are
fine—all their feathers returned.
The four ladies said that to forgive
you have to eat a lot of protein
to gain back your strength.
They said to drink as many
glasses of water as the hours
you are awake. And I'm
supposed to tell her that and
that nothing looks like a monster
and that her hair is not thin
as two shoestrings.

Elijah

When you open the door
he humps the banister. He drinks
so little from the cup so little so
everyone can't be sure if
he's really there or not but
it doesn't really matter. You don't
see him climb the chimney, slide
down the roof, it is slate, and into
the open window upstairs. He looks
so pretty in your dresses while
you help wash the dishes
downstairs. He waits for you to
come up, brush your teeth, climb
into bed and onto him. You
crush his arm and it doesn't
matter either. Next year he will be
elsewhere but tonight this night
you're the winner. It's a big night
when you're sleeping with Elijah.

Ella

By the time you get this the cat
will have been dead one week.
I am sorry. I was in the hills I
had brought a picnic for myself.
Driving home it was snowing.
Surprising for May on
the kind of day that also allowed
for a picnic, like I said. There
were two ways home and
I didn't take the freeway. Once I
drove from Missouri to
Minnesota on the freeways
in a snowstorm. Now I take
smaller roads. Better to be
slow on a slow road than
slow on a fast road where the
fools might forget it's snowing.
And on the slow road there was a
wall of snow, like in a cartoon
where the rain is on one side of
the street and not the other.
The wall was so thick and
tall. I was stuck there it
snowed for four days and
no one came, everyone
must have gone the other way.
This is all to say that when
I came home on Wednesday

the cat was dead. Near the
back door. I am so sorry.
I hope you can forgive me and
accept this kitten in a box. She
should wake up in a day or two,
they just gave her something to
ease the journey. I had
the postman put lots of
Fragile stamps on the
box. I didn't name her—I
thought I'd let you do it. Send
me pictures when you do.

Emmy

Jesus Christ can help—he
is the right answer. There
are days when it seems
that nothing is going the
way it's supposed to and
your friend's mother's in the
hospital and you can't find
your shoes and then your aunt's
in the hospital and it's
raining trees outside. And you try
to say enough is enough
without sounding redundant.
But then Harvey, the pilot, is
so nice—why is he so happy?
One hour and ninety-four minutes of
flight time he said. People aren't
usually so happy. Let us just pray
for a safe journey of few
bumps. I can see straight
into the ear next to me a good
inch and a half into this man's
head. Fabulous. Truly. Just
send it all on to Jesus.

Enoch

Like Elijah he doesn't
die supposedly. He
and Elijah always argue.
Elijah gets all the attention.
Families want ghosts
to entertain at birthday
parties and Elijah takes
all the jobs even though he
doesn't need the money.
Being the more important
ghost, god provides for him.
But Enoch swims every day and
that is one thing that makes him
happy. He likes to swim in
all the rivers. It is comforting
and Elijah is afraid of water so
Enoch can't be bothered there.
The creatures in the waters haven't
met Elijah and they think of Enoch
often. Enoch and the Loch Ness Monster.

Feivel

There was this movie maybe you've seen
it. It is called *An American Tail*. The tail
part is funny because it is a pun on tale as
in a story and tail as in a mouse
because the movie is about a mouse with
a tail named Feivel. The mouse not the tail.
I have thought about Feivel and that movie
recently. Recently I was at a wedding shower
and the bride wanted and received flip
flops that said "Just Mauied" on their bottoms
so that if you walk in them on the
sand everyone will see. And in the movie
there was an older lady mouse with a
speech impediment she said mauied for
married and when I saw the flip flops I
remembered mauied—but from where—
so I repeated it and soon I saw the old
lady mouse in my mind. I am sure
the movie came before the flip flops.
You can only really wear those
flip flops if you're going to Hawaii. It
would be silly to wear them in Florida.

If my mother's best friend were a doll
with a string to pull for a repetition
she would say I hate Florida. Many
people in Florida have had face lifts and
breast augmentations. It is fantastically

scary. *An American Tail* is also scary
because this little mouse named Feivel
is separated from his family on their way
from Russia to America. They had to leave
because of anti-Semitism. *Maus I* and *II*
are also stories in which mice face
anti-Semitism. There are many
Jewish people in Florida. I am
Jewish but I haven't had any breast
augmentation. If I haven't had
any breast augmentation or a
face lift then I am not from Florida.
It is scary to be a little mouse far
from your family because mice
are smaller than people and everything
is so much farther. Dogs were used in the
Holocaust by the Nazis to scare the Jews
and dogs are scary in *An American Tail*.
Many Jewish people don't have dogs. Some
do but many don't. In Israel my sister says
there are so many cats and no dogs because
they were scary. Dog is to Jew as cat is to
mouse. My mother is afraid of dogs but she
was not in the Holocaust. I am frightened
by big ones but now that I'm taller I'm less
afraid because the jumping is less high
relative to my face. A dog can jump much
higher than a mouse but mice are also scary.
Except Feivel. He was a nice Jewish
mouse who missed his family. I miss
my family. They are not mice but I
miss them. In the end Feivel and his

family are reunited. I haven't found
my family yet but Feivel has and he
taught us all never to stop looking
even if we aren't looking for
mice. It works for everything.

Ferdinand

My dictionary of names has a
huge entry on Ferdinand but
they don't mention the book
by that name about the bull—it
has a red cover and it is written
by Munro Leaf who also authored
How to Behave and Why. The latter
is a book I always want to give to
small children I know but never
do. It would seem rude I think.
Recently, I found something that
I composed when I was seven or
eight. It seems most appropriate
for this occasion of Ferdinand.

Once there lived a hunter from Connecticut
that hunted in New Hampshire. He always
asked himself, should I bring an extra
bullet or no? The answer was always yes.
This is where he liked to shoot: by the brook,
where the bull sat, eating a cookie. Actually,
he would walk over to the bush and aim. In
his spare time he went over to an oak tree
and nibbled at a cookie. His head was full of
ideas but there was one empty space and that
would have included: when you start to
doze off the bull comes charging at you!

Fifi

I.

Colored windows in the
city where the nannies
walk the babies tend
to break when the
Yankees beat the
Red Sox. Johnny
Damon is so pretty
with his long hair
and his protein
did you see how
he struck and broke
the bat? I can tell
you with assurance
that this time it
will be different—both
the Red Sox and
John Kerry will
prevail. How good it
is to be from
Massachusetts
in October when
both apples and
small ponies make
good livings. Have
you seen the painter
Nancy how her

brush strokes are
so tiny you
would think she
uses toothpicks for
paintbrushes. Nancy's
husband is a Mormon
he was born and
raised in Utah but
his business took
him all the way
to Boston. Mostly
everyone is Gentile
and the sky is
not as open but still
somehow he can
better love his Nancy.
If John Kerry
beats the Yankees
then the Red Socks
will be happy
oh those Yankees
are as bad
as Mr. Bush. What a
good day it would
be for Massachusetts
if they won
first the Pats then
the Sox then
John Kerry.

II.

Paris Hilton and
her sister, the less
hot one, were elected.

The Red Sox
still won. At
least we have
them at least
we have sox.

Geraldine

Today is not a day to be pregnant.
The environs are such that
anything could result in an
anti-pregnancy. The air
pressure makes a
fetus impossible. On
airplanes especially. Once,
I was driving, trying not to
get pregnant in Missouri and
the billboard this one billboard
in northern Missouri almost
Iowa said if you think you're
fat now, wait until you're
pregnant. For the most part
the roads there are for
truckers who all go home
and tell their wives and
girlfriends and daughters.
I went home I am not
a trucker and I laughed
at Missouri and Iowa for
where they are. A face and
its belly a big belly in
the middle of the country.
Missouri is always pregnant.

Gwenda

Go back to school
and read "Ceridwen" there.
When you finish, buy
Carwyn flowers. When
you give her them
tell her she is beautiful
more beautiful than the
others. Take a picture
of the moment for other
moments later when she
will have forgotten. Finally,
adopt several small
children and teach them
everything you learned in
school the second time.
Give them words for their
birthdays and lower case
letters every afternoon
with a snack.

Haskel

We were. Well we
tried calling. The
forklift operator said
no, but next time. We
forgot several letters
we used to know
and it was upsetting.
Do you say iodine?
What about the
constellations, have
you found them?
I am reading a
book about the
stars and why.
And who is there.
Orange. Orange who.
Orange you going
to come in. She said
pick the very best one
and it is her—hands down,
which means hands
down motherfucker
it's all over. Here
I made these bags
for you. She makes
bags and machine
washes them and then
people buy them and

the money goes some
place good for a
good thing. Good
is where the ocean
is here I'll show you.

Heddwyn

Carwyn meets
Ceridwen on an
undisclosed corner
in a designated city.
They discuss things
like baseball and
the food network
and the recent
elections and social
graces like the art
of holding doors
for others. They
both wear good
comfortable shoes
because the talk
is long and
there are no
chairs in the
city and it will
be a long walk
home. All their
friends are poets and
they all like to
discuss everything.
They are the
angels of their
communities they
wear white often

like every day is
a wedding and
they are the brides,
fair, that means pretty,
and blessed therefore holy.

Helmet

Helmet is a tiny
whale that swims
inside the sea.
And everywhere that
Helmet goes the
sea is blue and
green. Helmet has sweet
eyes and smooth skin
and a big tail for
such a small whale.

A tiny whale is a pretty
new phenomenon
they are still a secret in
the sea but they will be sold
in exotic pet shops one day
like how miniature
watermelons are so hot
and so expensive these days.

But Helmet the tiny whale. He
swims hard and small each day
he sleeps and eats little fish
one fish per meal. I don't know
how many meals a day for a
whale a tiny whale.
If you asked Helmet how he
was, he would say—just fine—

his voice warbling birds
and some part chuckle
blowing bubbles for
the likes of all of us.

Isadore

I thought this
was a girl's
name. A girl's
name on the
side of a truck
somewhere
in Michigan a
truck we passed.

A trucking
company named
for a woman a strong
woman named
Isadore who
could lift many
boxes. Isa short
for Isadore, a
woman on the
side of a truck
in Michigan.
Isa the truck
named Isadore.

In Canada
near Michigan I
bought this
book because of
Isadore a

woman named
Isadore made me
do this. But then
Isabel becomes
Isaiah and later
Isidora and
Isidore neither
of whom
I wanted.

Isadore
is nowhere
to be found a
delightful Cajun
fisherman a
boy's name
definitely an
Asian fellow,
deceased,
bringing us some
much needed rain.
Isadore is
a door is next
a delightful
fisherman a
professor of
music even more
blasphemy the
patron saint of
farmers and large
gardens is on
her way is a

nice old man
still affecting
the south a
social cripple
wreaking havoc
with my sinuses
a retired high
school principal
spinning around
in the Gulf
of Mexico.

Isadore II

Your tongue is green
his knee is green and

green is green. My
soap is green

it smells like green
the walls are green

for you especially.
Isadore are you

for me are you
soft or white can

you count well.
There is a lot

of arithmetic here.
Green comes and

goes as it pleases,
has a key in its mouth.

Green is the keynote
speaker at this year's

star gazers' convention.

It is my hero. Green

tells me things, things
like my hair is nice

the way it smells. I
use green shampoo

I say. Isadore
can you count the

green in the room how
many greens does

it take to take to
cross the road.

Johanna

His wife is an elegant room.

Cameo white with green things of detail.

Orange helps the eyes in a couple of ways. Carrots. Signs.

The room is beautiful. So many syllables. Argentina.

His wife is dutiful. Elegant. Roomy. On the first floor
to the left of the stairs.

His wife like many things needs to be cleaned and
ventilated, is glad when well lit.

Kaapo

He runs a baby factory
in the shed. I bought
Theo, my now-dead,
there. One hundred
plus twenty dollars.
His blue face
was so endearing.

Socket teeth. I
fight myself about
out of season things.
Boots, fruit, leaves.
Babies. A page to
a page minus one
is how much.

Kaapo is a great
businessman. He
is slow to return
calls. An extraordinary
bullshitter. Lives at
home with his parents.
Pays rent for the
shed. The shed
that is painted.

Babies here. Good
price. Quiet ones.

Big ones. Girl
ones. Cash or
check only. Payable
to Kaapo's Backyard
Babies.

Theo's death was
short. Jews bury quick.
Good to the body.
Theo died in the
morning and was
buried the next one.
My uncle sat with
him all night. Jews
keep the dead
company. Even
in hospitals it is
done. They understand.
Hospitals are good
places if you ask nice.

Karp

Like fruit from Russia it
was difficult not to
desire her. She was truly a
lovely ripe peach, nectarine,
whatever. Like a hurricane
he ate when he was hungry.
A fish-fruit would be good
for the body. Sweet protein.
On a corner across from a
baseball field please. Cooked
well this dish would benefit
from a glass of water. Even
if it doesn't pay well I am
going to drive a fruit truck
from the country to the other
country. Gentle. Gentle they
tell me over unpaved roads.
Use a pencil to test the skins
when stopping for gas. Fruit
and gas have had big roles in
dreams this year. Serenade me
slow. I promise to respond
within four to six months.

Laz

This was going to be
about this kid Tara
and I knew named Laz, short
for Lazarus. It was going
to be for Tara and about
the kid. But rather
to try not and tell any story
about blue or your mother or
how you can be so
terrible. We tried hard
and didn't make it. That
is not a story, not even close.

Leander

A blooming lake was
born hours ago. A
quiet place in a big
sea. Animals you have
ever seen float there.
How everyone likes to
talk about the states
of animals. In water
animals might float
or swim. Or die.
Dogs walk and swim.
Frozen water bowls
in the snow. And lovely
teeth. Just like when
we were all smaller then.

Lech

A fever on
Wednesday
makes waste
on Thursday I'll
call but I
know you'll
never get there.
The monsters in
the city are so
big and bad and
pretty did you
hear the chief
making language
—in specific?!!
China, he said, in
specific. Pacifically,
China is located.
Perhaps the president
is really British, one
accent wearing another.
My sister lives abroad
and she says Brits
forget Pacific for specific
all the time. When
your name is Lech you
have some choices.
Hard or soft or throaty.

Meinwen

Read "Ceridwen"
twice more. Once
while someone else
is talking. Then try
singing it to the fishes.

Mitrofan

The engines go home
every day like everyone
else. Remove outerwear
to become comfortable
in living rooms. Sully
calls Mike to talk shit
about his boss how
breaks are shorter
now and oil is
increasingly tasteless.
Sometimes on weekends
Mike and Sully take
the girls out for the
night. They've been
to the opera a few times.
The girls love the opera.
Sully and Mike like
the opera too but mostly
for its big fancy dresses.

Montserrat

A lady's name also
a place in Spain I've
seen but the lady
with a name
like Jagged Hill,
please, touch my
jagged breasts and my
jagged hair. Nope,
haven't found her yet. If
you find her first be
sure to have some
planting gloves on.
There is no such
thing as being
too nice to a woman
named that. She
is lonely and has
many rough places.

Myrtle

Myrtle me myrtle you.
Myrtle is a plant
too—Sophie is only
a name. Myrtle may
be any noun. Myrtle
the beach. Myrtle the
plant. Myrtle the lady
—she is myrtle too.
Myrtle will be married
and green and warm.

Nan

Nan would like this
photograph of a
donkey being checked
for explosives. She
would laugh and then
say something both
smart and true.

Nan is so smart she could
solve crossword puzzles
on your back but she
might think it tasteless
and it might be.

I think Nan
has a box of
poems somewhere
and I know that
she likes ice cream.

She would love
this picture. A bomb
in a donkey. Quick.
Call the save the
donkeys foundation.

In this photograph Nan is
not the donkey nor is she the
explosives detector nor the
wand itself. She is not the
donkey's owner, nor the owner's
wife. But she could be
the patron behind the donkey—
the person waiting to get through.

Naomi

Spanish soap and
Dial soap were
walking through a
forest when the
spirit jumped out
from the bushes.

Where are you going?
Aruba they say.
For what?
We bought a
timeshare they say.
Take me with you.
How much do you
weigh—there's a
weight limit. I don't
eat much. Okay. Let's
see. Come into my
purse. There. Perfect.

The spirit fits into
the side compartment
and weighs almost
nothing. Dial soap and
Spanish soap and the
secret spirit all go
to Aruba for two weeks
in February. The end.

Norbert

Don't let them get you
down so Norbert. Keep

that fire, your
belly that fire in

the belly keep it
fed. Take yourself

north, Norbert, far
far away from this.

Make yourself safe
find a house up there

Norbert be so
happy for yourself and

the trucks that go
that far. Norbert you have

so much trucks behind
you so much trucks

hauling so much
boxes of love.

Oded

To say you like
something to say
a lot, to speak
a long time about
this. To make
a thing you
like a thing for
another. To say
find this thing
the next time you
find yourself looking.
To say nice, this
thing, a friend, a
man, a man a
nice man. To
say thank you, say
thank you thing
I like for this.

Ollie

"Happy Valentimes"
to everybody.

And then in came
the forest tromping
through the first
floor parlor.

Pancrazio

I went to church
with my friend in
Gramercy Park and
it was a slow hour.
I'm too Jewish
to receive communion.
She says the big
difference between
church and temple
is that Catholics keep
their coats on and
Jews take them off.

She fell asleep in
the pew, coat on like a
sleeping bag. Mine
was off and beside me.
When they kneeled I sat
as far forward as I
could so the man
behind me couldn't
rest his praying head
on my back. I'm also
too Jewish to kneel.
Just to think that
people keeping their
coats on and Jesus,
etc., comes from so

many years of people
taking their jackets
off and hanging them
up in coat rooms.

Sometimes I am
so unlike myself.
A big runny nose
walks around a city
nobody likes him.
The nose falls in the
market and no one
picks him up. Just like
that Jesus, everybody
hates me.

Pansy

This was the moment
that no one had been
waiting for. The
flight attendant
stepped up to
the bat. Delivered
the speech unmercifully.
Back at home
she answered fan
mail like it was
her religion. Wore
a green wedding
dress. What language
do you speak, she
asked everyone. She
was a visionary of
sorts. Asserted
her legs firmly in
the park. Unafraid
of the night and
its colors she
would count as
much as she wanted.
She sent some flowers
to the moon received
an illegible yet

warm thank you
the following day.

All of this is
to say that
good comes where
you let it come. When
the state policemen come
to your front door and
offer to install an escalator
to the moon make
sure you let them.

Peninnah

There's so little for
this place. A few
sandwiches and
some coffee and
free refills and then
her church (was
Catholic) and my
church consisted of
a dark room of sad
people. Do you
like my picture
map? I bought it
for myself with eight
dollars. We went to
Greenwich Village
where we did not see
any of my heroes.
We saw some
people but none
of them smiled.
Teeth in that
city can be
more special the
most special of
anything. Wear
them in your
mouth or find them
in the sink of a

fancy restaurant's
washroom. That
bitch punched the
other one's teeth
out and left them
in the sink right there.
Who would try
smiling after that.

Quinton

The queen isn't
the real queen.
The real queen
is a man held
up in a room.
The queen we see
is the real queen's
sister. The real
queen sits in
a tower a ways
away from the
castle and plays
video games.
Consumes many
soft drinks.
There is a hole
in the floor of
his favorite room
and sometimes for
fun he sticks his
head inside just
to make sure it
still fits.

Rella

I wish I didn't
talk so much. So
many evenings and
me saying to myself
Oh Rella why'd you
have to go and
say so much. Why
couldn't you have
let them say
something more. Huh?
They seemed so
lovely together. I
just had to say
so. And the food.
I thought they
would have to cart
me out of there
wiping my face
up with a rag.
Sometimes when I'm
walking through a
crowd in a room
my brain closes—my
eyes are still open
but I can't see
one shape to save
myself or my feet.
The sound cuts too—

and everything slows—
like a movie. I
find my love in the
third stall and we
make sex right
there in the ladies
room of a popular
restaurant. Yes. That
is how it happened.
That is everything.

Rhonwen

For the last time for
god's sake I'm not
telling you again.
Read Carwyn. Read
it so hard you can
read it backwards.

Runa

Ready and waiting is
pretty or is pretty or
is awed by the
fisherman is an outdated
version is a bad
mother here. Is
ready and waiting
for your pretty or
is looking good
going to wrestlemania.
She is the
advanced Maryland
automatic network
disk archiver is very
clear. She is
currently having a
small rebellion against
the sheer amount of
world. She is 5
stories and tall and
one of the oldest buildings
in my city. She is to
instrument as large
volume of ice is to
you. She is in good
company wearing her
mini dress in purple.
She is designed to

handle a large number
of vacation days. She
is a detector being
constructed at the
South Pole. A
film about an
extraordinary horse
named Biddle. A detector
being constructed
she is a film
about an extraordinary
horse and a boy
named Biddle.
She is an incredible
example of what people
with a hearing loss
can accomplish with
the right kind of
support, exactly
14 minutes old in this
picture. She is
no exception eating
super blue green
algae. Totally
useless is a little
panda bear who
lives in the forest.
Is one great cookie.
Ready and waiting.
The mice were Jews
cats were Nazis
pigs were Poles and

dogs were Americans.
She is queen of
backups is also
a mommy is
currently having a
small rebellion against
the sheer size
11 pounds 4 ounces.
She is an ache
is ready and waiting
for a detector being
constructed at the
South Pole. She
is 5 stories tall
and seeded 7 at
Toronto ready and
waiting currently
having a small rebellion.

Sanna

When you meet a
greedy man on an
airplane do you say
excuse me, sir, could
you please keep to
your side of the
armrest or do you
let him take your
pretzels and two
cans of orange juice
and keep touching your
side with his elbow?
At the end of
all of this, I am
still without a real
sense of math or
time and I am still
not sure which
market I should
frequent. I keep
by mistake saying
to my one-eyed
friend how all these
one-eyed men on
the online dating
service I use want
to meet for something
and I'm not interested.

It's too hard to go
back to where we were
ten minutes ago, etc.
Somewhere today
an airplane will land
and someone who lost
a lot of gasoline over
some ocean will win a
piece of history. PETA,
etc., will be there with
pitchforks on the tarmac.
No, we don't test on
animals anymore. No,
I don't need to see the
ocean to know where
I am in Massachusetts.
Massachusetts is more
honest than Minnesota.
Sometimes they are called
Massholes but at least
they don't scratch
themselves under the
tray table on the
airplane. Next to me
this asshole from
Minnesota scratches
himself under the safety
of the tray table that
is to be stowed during
the landing which is
soon and when I say "himself"
I'm not referring to his "leg."

Maybe in Massachusetts
we would all be different.
Jennifer Lopez is not
from Massachusetts but
she is so honest she doesn't
want a fashion show to
be "too real" she wants
magic like the movies.
I'll be straight with you
I watched her program
two and a half times. And
I didn't used to floss too
often but my friend just
discovered eight cavities
so now I do it as much
as I can stand. Soon
Massachusetts will be
the president of this
place and we will all
be honest with such
beautiful teeth and
a sense of water. It
makes you honest I
swear. Good people
are honest and good
people floss often—
they tell us to floss often
and drink lots of water.

Sylvie

Sylvie is a girl in a
poem I once wrote. The
poem was called "The
House Dress" and it
was about "William and
Sylvia" who "live in all of
the villages in Dublin."
Then there is something
of a distraction to get
to the part where I say
"Bill once met a woman
with only one nostril—
she was born that
way. Her name was Helen
and Helen had been with
another woman named Helen
and both of their last
names were Shaffer."
And I explain how
they were not "one person"
but they were two. The only
difference "though was the
nostril—Helen's nostril." I'm
so funny sometimes. And then
it ends: "Will and
Sylvie thank god for
the both of theirs when
they remember before going

to bed." Sylvie is just
another way of saying Sylvia
like how Bill and Will are for
William. But like I said Helen
and Helen are different. Check
their noses if you don't believe me.

Tadhg

I don't know if it's
you didn't get
the prescriptions
or you make me feel
like I'm nobody
but something is coming from
the other room and the
intonation isn't happy. I
would have *responded* better
if you had *asked* nicer.
That sort of thing.

There are two kinds
of people: those who
are never surprised
and those who are often.

Los sensitivos everywhere
are crying themselves
to sleep. You
were sick and I wrapped
you in women's
clothes when we ran
out of blankets.

Swallow each of
these with a big
glass of your favorite

clear liquid. The
green one brings
back memory. The
blue one is for
happiness. Yellow
is for a clean house.
And pink is for
more pink tomorrow.

You can teach a
fish to eat a cow but
you can't teach it
to swim. It either
does or it doesn't.

Ughtred

I wish I could tell you
how it might be to live
in Maine and then
somewhere else for a while.
Mother says there's no real
difference between right here
and New Hampshire except
that here we have a house
and so it's free.

Most times I'm just going
about my business and someone
up and asks "What are you
going to do" and that means
"What are you going to
do with yourself that I might
consider important." My
mother thinks I should
get a shaggy kind of
haircut and that's a
short-term plan. I'll do that
next week. I think that
I am beginning to lose my
hair because my head
always hurts. After the
short-term plan I
would like to have children

and someday cowboy boots.
If I had money soon I
could afford the boots
and telling you about
these ladies over here they
are so happy about some
story where a man on
a cell phone got into an
accident and when
everyone got out of their
cars two old ladies started
to hit him, for the cell
phone I guess. One with
a Bible and one with an
umbrella.

I am a real good listener.
If I had more money I
could listen for you and
tell you how these other people
here are the assholes, such assholes
that I won't tell one of them that
his lights are still on. If I had
more money I could tell you
how this lady asshole needs
a place to live a place
to live with her dog and
boyfriend named Neil and
when she was younger she
had her own telephone line
and would get prank calls.

What are you wearing, etc.,
and she told them,
not knowing any better.

It is still early in the
morning and all I can say is
I wish myself a pretty pair
of cowboy boots and
even prettier pregnancy.

Virág

Like a name like
flower. Like a
country like the
sound of a state.
Once we drove
in a small car
through a field of
tulips so red so
red the sky had
to leave. The sky
was not itself and
all that was left
was gray so gray
that red could
seem more red
than anything. That
day so many cars
stopped, people
ran into the
field and made
intonations to the
tulips. It was
February. A good
month for tulips.
In a small country
with a view of
the ocean.

Wilberforce

Somewhere lady things
become man things
somehow in Ohio.
Ohio has a perfectly
small voice and with it
Ohio invites you to visit.
The rest stops along
the highway in Ohio
are unisexual. Ladies
and gentlemen may
all have an equal
opportunity to eat
and drink and make
use of the facilities. I
think there are
farms in Ohio.
I can't quite
remember but I
think there are farms.
I don't know things
about trucks or
horses or birds and I
don't imagine many
things will change any
time soon. But I've been
to many small towns
in Ohio. Miss Ohio
became Miss America

last year, back when
the pageant still had a
talent component. Miss
Ohio sang improv. She
asked the audience
for three words that were
like Ohio and she
made up a song
right there on
national television in
front of all the judges.
Someone shouted
Drew Carey. Someone
else said Iowa, another
state with an overabundance
of vowels. One person
offered Amish people.
Miss Ohio sang a song
about Drew living in
Iowa as an Amish person
and the audience loved
it and the judges loved it
even more. The judges
were Amish too. Once
crowned Miss America,
Miss Ohio traveled
to all the rest stops along
the interstate in Ohio to
meet all the other Americans.
Rest stops I know about. I know
that sometimes there's
ice cream and sometimes

there are donuts. I know
that it's best not to
go into the stores
unless you want to
walk away empty
handed having just
spent $14.95 on
a t-shirt that will never
be worn. And I know that
you can never take
enough napkins back
with you to keep in the
glove box. You never know
when you might have an accident.

Xavier

Hannah knows
that I tend to
prefer repetition
and Hannah knows
someone who is
named Xzavier
with a "z." Hannah's
name repeats itself
it is a palindrome.
Hannah and I repeatedly
search for a special kind
of cheese so she can make
a special kind of soup
and so we go to all the
Mexican supermarkets
and one of them plays
loud music so loud that
we refer to it now as
"dance party supermarket."
The only other Xavier I
know is Xavier Roberts and
he is the father of my cabbage
patch doll. She is the first
thing I named and her name
is Shulie Baby. Shulie
Baby, like all other
cabbage patch dolls,
is branded on her bottom

with Xavier's signature
in green. I think it is
disgusting, but where else
might he have signed? The
foot. The belly. It is Xavier's
sole purpose to sign every
doll before it is put into
a box. Hannah knows a lot
of people and Hannah knows
a girl and the girl's parents
thought it would be funny
to likewise brand her
with their names. The
girl's parents' names,
Susan and George so and so,
are permanently fixed on
her right buttock and Susan
and George so and so did it
when the girl was still a baby,
like how some parents pierce
their children's ears early
so it won't hurt later. I
would never do that to my
children. I would do it later
so that they could better
remember how it was.

Yseult

She lost her
imagination
to a toilet in the
Czech Republic.
It had been
resting just a
moment on her
bag balanced on
top of the toilet
paper dispenser.
Tragically, turning
to kick the flusher
with her foot her
hip knocked the
bag to the floor but
the other went down
the toilet already
spinning. She still
has not left the
country. She
refuses to leave
without it. She
only hopes that
it likewise wants
her back and if so
hasn't forgotten what
she looks like. It
was never very good
at remembering.

Zeb

I remember you as
something of a
small thing wanting
to come in and over.

Something of a
thunderstorm you wanted
to come in and over.
Sorry, my Aunt said no.

A thunderstorm you wanted
for your birthday and I'm
sorry my Aunt said no.
How about some berries?

For your birthday I'm
going to go too.
How about some berries
for the drive back?

Going to go to
Alaska. Will you come
for the drive back?
I promise no singing.

Alaska, will you come
to Maine for the summer?
I promise no singing
but I'd like you to come

to Maine for the summer
my family will be there
and I'd like you to come.
It's a long drive but

my family will be there
and they want to meet you.
It's a long drive but
they like Bob Dylan.

And they want to meet you
they are from Minnesota.
They like Bob Dylan
he sings so small and big.